ERWIN ROMMEL: PHOTOGRAPHER

VOLUME 3:

ADVENTURES IN COLOR

ERWIN ROMMEL: PHOTOGRAPHER

VOLUME 3: *ADVENTURES IN COLOR*

by Erwin Rommel & Zita Steele

FLETCHER & CO. PUBLISHERS

www.fletcherpublishers.com

NOTE: The photographs in this collection belonged to Erwin Rommel before they were seized from his widow by U.S. military forces during the final stages of World War II. Rommel, an avid photographer, intended to author another book on military strategy if he survived the war. Some of these photos he took to illustrate his strategy and maneuvers, while others were for his personal interest. To the best of my knowledge, all photos were taken by Rommel unless he is shown in a picture taken by someone else, either an unidentified German war photographer or close personal associate.

DISCLAIMER: This book does not in any way promote Nazi ideology. In addition, Rommel was never a member of the Nazi party, nor was he responsible for any war crimes or genocide.

Erwin Rommel: Photographer
—*Volume 3: Adventures in Color*

By Erwin Rommel & Zita Steele
Fletcher & Co. Publishers
© September 2016, Fletcher & Co. Publishers LLC.

Cataloging-in-Publication data for this book is available from the Library of Congress.
Library of Congress Catalog Number 2015960902

Photographer & Illustrator: Erwin Rommel
Author, Editor & Illustrator: Zita Steele
Interior design: Noël Fletcher
Photos of Zita Steele by Noël Fletcher
First Edition
Published in the United States of America

Cataloging information
ISBN-10: 1-941184-11-1
ISBN-13: 978-1-941184-11-0

Contents

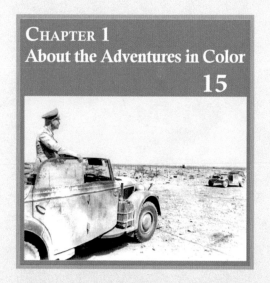

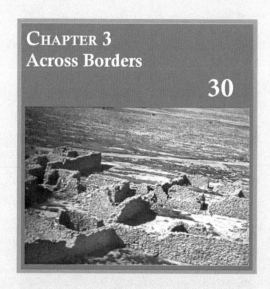

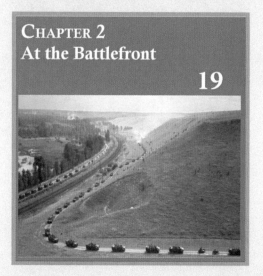

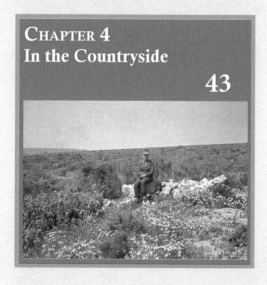

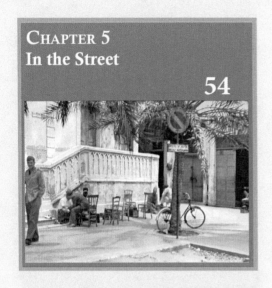

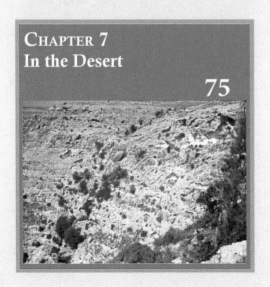
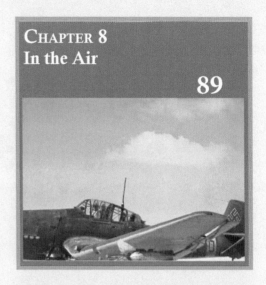
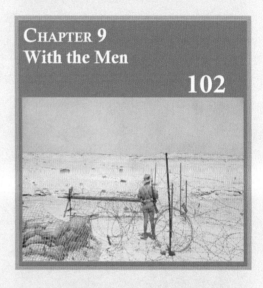

This Series

Photography was one of Field Marshal Erwin Rommel's favorite pastimes. Between 1940 and 1942, he took thousands of photos. These images cover a wide variety of subjects reflecting both Rommel's military and personal interests. Rommel was meticulous in labeling his photos. He intended many of these pictures to be illustrations in a manual on military tactics that he planned to write after World War II. His untimely death prevented him from doing so.

Rommel also collected pictures of himself taken by German war photographers and others. Rommel evidently saved the images to document or remember important events in his life. These photos are interspersed throughout each book in the series.

My goal in the *"Erwin Rommel: Photographer"* series is to provide readers an opportunity to gain insights about Rommel through both the photos he took and those he collected. The photos are presented to provoke thought and allow people to make their own interpretations. The series offers a unique perspective on Rommel, while providing a glimpse of what he experienced and saw in the war.

The first book, *"Volume I: A Survey,"* contains a broad overview of Rommel's photographic work and a sampling of overarching themes in his collection. The other books explore individual themes in greater detail.

VOLUME 3: ADVENTURES IN COLOR

Color photography was rare in Rommel's time, particularly since color film was more difficult to develop than black-and-white. He deliberately used color photography to capture images he wanted to preserve due to their significance as well as to retain the vivid colors of the subjects.

Rommel seems to have intended most of these photos for personal use. Images such as those of Bedouins, flowers, palm trees, and other officers were clearly taken by him as mementos. A few images show he handed his camera to another person so as to appear in particular pictures. Some photos, such as those of battles or military vehicles, may have been intended for military documentation.

The subjects in Rommel's color images are slightly different from those in his black-and-white photography. Familiar themes in Rommel's photography include nature, his soldiers, and machinery. New themes include cultural elements, places and other subjects. (The themes are categorized in the chapters of this book.)

Most of these photos were taken in North Africa in 1941 and 1942. Other photos appear to have been taken in Belgium and France in 1940, with additional family photos taken in Austria during 1942 while Rommel had sick leave from the war in North Africa.

ROMMEL'S ILLUSTRATIONS

"Alle sind wie gelähmt." Rommel and his men surprise a group of enemy
soldiers near the border of Slovenia in 1917, who immediately surrendered.

Freehand drawing was one of Rommel's favorite hobbies since childhood. He used his talent at sketching to create images and maps to illustrate his experiences during World War I. Some of these were scenes from memory. Others are tactical sketches that Rommel took great trouble to create. Not long after WWI ended in 1918, Rommel, in his late 20s, traveled to former battlefields on a motorcycle with his wife and a bulky camera in tow. He used photographs to draw detailed maps.

It proved difficult to reconstruct his battle experiences in narrative detail. The final product of his work, a manual called *"Infantry Attacks,"* was published many years later in 1937. The development of compact handheld cameras in the 1930s made things much easier for Rommel—he planned to use photographs as illustrations for his next military book, which his death prevented him from completing.

Rommel's WWI sketches, made in pen and ink, contain the same visual techniques he used in his photography, such as symmetry, layering and texturing. Many of these similarities are apparent when the drawings are compared to his color photos.

The drawings included in this book are rare. The originals—along with maps, writings and photographs—were kept in a trunk at Rommel's house and were stolen by American G.Is in 1945. Rommel's illustrations in this book are from an old damaged German edition of *"Infantry Attacks"* that is no longer in print. As with the photographs in this series, I digitally restored the drawings without altering Rommel's work.

My Approach to These Photos

As a graphic artist and writer, I am well aware of the power and intrinsic ability of images to convey information using visual elements that are stronger than printed words. Images, however, can be distorted through various means, such as cropping and design manipulations. In this manner, photographs, especially in this digital age, can be taken out of context, altered from the original image, or slanted to show a different viewpoint contrary to the intent of the photographer.

One of the most important goals of my restoration was to preserve the photographer's original work. The contents of the images have not been cropped out of context or distorted in any way.

All photos taken by Rommel are shown in full frame, as they actually appeared when he captured the shot. For some photos, I have extracted close-up sections

To create this book, I delved through hundreds of photos, slides, negatives, and photographic contact prints in these boxes at the National Archives where Rommel's personal photos are stored after having been seized by American forces during World War II.

and placed them next to Rommel's full-frame images so readers can see interesting details I observed in certain areas of the pictures.

The only photos which have been cropped are those taken by others of Rommel himself. This was done to make it easier for viewers to see Rommel clearly, particularly in pictures of him surrounded by other people. In some cases, I have extracted close-ups of Rommel, cropped them to provide greater visibility of him, and placed them next to the original photos of himself.

Rommel used a Leica camera for much of his photography. While the exact model is unknown, the Leica III D camera was popular during World War II. Rommel's camera and accessories were stolen after his death from his home in Germany by American soldiers, who even took his uniforms.

ROMMEL'S IMAGES & MY PHOTO RESTORATION

The Counterintelligence Corps of the U.S. military seized Rommel's photo collection in 1945 from his widow in Germany. They confiscated his Leica equipment and thousands of photos that he had taken, including color images.

Unfortunately not all the color images confiscated from the Rommel home were preserved in the National Archives—many disappeared between the time of confiscation and the time the material was donated to the Archives, and were likely stolen by American G.I.s.

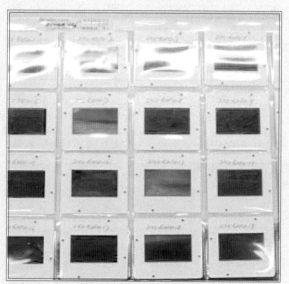

Rommel's son Manfred said his father's color collection contained thousands of photos; however, the color photos in the National Archives number in the hundreds, and images described by Manfred are missing.

While examining the photos at the National Archives, I placed the color slides on the table before scanning the images.

Rommel's black-and-white images are crammed in boxes, while the color images have been preserved in slide format and kept in a vault to prevent decomposition.

Like the majority of Rommel's photographs, the color slide images are badly damaged. In most cases, the images are scratched, blotted, yellowed or darkened with age. Most have severe cases of "color casting"—unnatural discoloration which taints entire images with strange hues.

Color casting is often found in old photographs and can be caused by improper chemical development or by deterioration of dyes over time.

I am responsible for the restoration of all the photos in this book. My graphic design and multimedia skills are central to my work as an author and artist. All the images in this book have undergone a painstaking digital-restoration process.

Unlike the photos in the first two volumes of this series, the color images were the most difficult for me to restore.

The restoration process took much longer and was more complex due to the challenges presented by the blotching and color-cast damage.

I used a multilayered approach to this restoration; I worked on each photo about five times. The process I used is described below:

■ *Color cast removed*—Some images contained multiple color casts, or unnatural shades caused by deterioration. To remove color casting, I used a four-step process of identifying and digitally correcting chemical imbalances in the images. This four-step process often needed repetition. I performed it on each photo at least twice.

■ *Repaired and lightened*—Many of the photos were very dark and had to be lightened in order to be visible. Scratches, dust particles, and stains were removed. In addition, many photos were covered with bright red blotches due to age damage. Some blotches were very large, while others were small and literally covered entire images. I removed the blotches using repair techniques.

■ *Hand-tinted*—In many cases, simply removing color casting was not enough to restore the original colors. I had to tint each image by hand using painting methods to recreate the accurate colors in Rommel's original images.

Three examples of my restoration work in the various phases are shown on the next page.

COLOR CAST REMOVED

Rommel's original photo (left). The same photo after my restoration (right).

REPAIRED & LIGHTENED

Rommel's original photo (left). The same photo after my restoration (right).

HAND-TINTED

Rommel's original photo (left). The same photo after my restoration (right).

1

About the

Adventures in Color

Rommel surveys the war-torn desert landscape from his vehicle.

Rommel was particularly proud of his color photography, according to his son Manfred. He sometimes took daring snaps in the middle of battle to get sensational combat images. Many photos were lost following the American invasion of Germany in 1945.

It is unknown when Rommel began documenting his wartime experiences in color. He planned to write a book on military tactics — similar to his World War I manual *"Infantry Attacks"* — which some of his black-and-white photos were intended to illustrate. However, the majority of the color photos in this collection seem intended for his personal use.

Rommel used Agfa products for his color photography. Agfa (Aktien-Gesellschaft für Anilin-Fabrikation) was a German-owned company, which in 1936 produced a color film product called Agfacolor Neu, Germany's answer to America's Technicolor film. Color film was expensive during Rommel's era and also difficult to develop.

Color film was in high demand in Germany both before and during World War II. Despite Agfa's efforts to match Technicolor's quality, the German color film industry developed slowly and advanced through trial and error during the war. Color film was a rare treat rather than a readily available commodity.

While Rommel used black-and-white film to quickly capture scenes that crossed his path, he made extra efforts to create color images. The rarity of color film required him to seek special opportunities to use it. He also likely had a limited supply of it on the frontlines.

Unlike his black-and-white snapshots, Rommel's color photos were taken when he had greater time and freedom to compose images. While he used lights and objects to form patterns in his black-and-white compositions, he used colors, textures and layered subject matter to form patterns in color compositions.

The characteristics of Rommel's color images are consistent with those in his black-and-white images. All reflect his trademark techniques of casting lone objects against vast backdrops, capturing apparent ironies, creating linear patterns, or balancing objects in the frame with mathematical precision.

Rommel's adventures in color photography allow the reader to see vibrant glimpses of what he witnessed during the World War II — life behind desert frontlines, views from his reconnaissance airplane, bustling seaports, rugged landscapes, and the faces of diverse people whose eyes met his camera lens.

The photos are accompanied by sketches drawn by Rommel. These rare illustrations echo the same techniques he used in photo composition, positioning people and objects within his camera lens. His sketches, like his photos, feature strong curving and layered lines and depict ordinary soldiers. They provide additional insights into Rommel's unique perspective as both a soldier and an artist.

In a letter to his wife, Lucie, Rommel discussed sending color film home from North Africa.

• March 31, 1942 •

"It's also very lovely up here, as the flowers are still all in full bloom.
I've made a color film and will send it home shortly."

German infantrymen ascend a mountain ridge during the Battle of Caporetto in 1917. (Rommel had no caption on this drawing.)

The illustration above shows a curving row cutting through the center of the mountainside. Three soldiers are positioned almost perfectly within the middle of the frame. Rommel uses this technique repeatedly in his photos—a dominant, curving diagonal line of some type appears in the middle of the image. Like this drawing, Rommel's photo compositions often show people centered within a frame and set against towering backdrops.

2

At the Battlefront

Rommel captured this aerial photo of tanks and troops in France. He took several black-and-white photos of these columns from his airplane, but this is the only known surviving color photo. It is likely he wanted to have both color and black-and-white images to use in a military strategy book he was preparing before he was murdered in 1944.

Rommel took a hands-on approach to military leadership. During battle, he led from the frontlines, motivating his troops under fire. He drove vehicles under fire and dodged bullets and bombs, often experiencing near misses.

During lulls in the fighting, Rommel constantly moved behind the lines. He surveyed his surroundings by land and air, inspected defenses, and mingled with ordinary soldiers at their battle posts. Talking with soldiers allowed him to gauge his men's morale. Personal visits from Rommel as commander also boosted their spirits.

Rommel had a lifelong interest in mathematics and mechanics; he loved building things and applied mathematical principles to daily problem solving. He analyzed battle fortifications, weapons, and vehicles. He often redesigned and invented military obstacles. He also devised new ways of using machines and material. He studied many of these things as he toured behind the frontlines.

Rommel stands in the center vehicle to survey events beyond the frame to the right. The occupants in his car and the one behind him all look towards the right. Tire tracks in the center of frame appear to be of the vehicle in which the photographer traveled ahead of Rommel.

Rommel was curious as well as active and had a tendency to go exploring. This sometimes placed him in danger. He had several harrowing experiences in North Africa after crossing into enemy territory.

A closeup of Rommel from the photo above.

The central focus of the image is a main building where men stand outside with a vehicle convoy parked in the middle. Palm trees dot the landscape in the upper frame. The linear angles of the walls, rows of men, and convoy combine with square buildings to form geometric shapes that dominate the image.

Rommel points his lens out an airplane window to preserve a camp scene with his troops in formation.

A windstorm raises clouds of sand high in the air as vehicles seek cover behind desert hills.

A sea of swirling tire tracks cut through the image in the foreground and middle ground. The tire patterns are balanced on each side by vehicles: four tanks (left) and trucks, including one with a white flag (right). Lonely figures of men stand in pairs near the trucks.

A sandy mist clouds the visibility of parked trucks and moving vehicles near the horizon. Rommel appears to have been overlooking the action while standing atop a hill, rather than from a plane, due to the proximity of the vegetation at the base of this photo.

A blurred image of a camp shows figures of men and dust clouds from moving vehicles.

The blurring of the image and angle indicates Rommel was in motion in a low-flying airplane when he took this photo. He composed this picture using one of his familiar techniques by horizontally layering the dirt road at the bottom, the greenbelt and brush hiding the trucks in the center, and dotted vehicles in the middle just below the horizon.

Rows of desert fortifications and fences form linear patterns that rise above the smooth surface of the ground below.

A single row of vehicles drives along a curving road at the base of a rocky hill.

The curving lines, position of moving vehicles within the frame, and stark backdrops in this photo have a similar look and feel to Rommel's photos of tank maneuvers near hills in France. The tip of his airplane window is visible in the upper right corner of the frame.

A battered vehicle lies destroyed and abandoned in the desert with its doors wide open and rocks covering its roof and hood.

This is a simple yet haunting image from the aftermath of an attack. Unlike other soldiers who took gory photos of victims and carnage, Rommel's wartime photograph avoids depictions of the dead. Only a few of his images show wounded German soldiers. Instead he expressed the toll of war in images with minimal subjects, which can have an eerie effect such as the vehicle above.

A tree hides the hood of Rommel's sleeping vehicle and obscures the view of his tent.

Rommel took this photo to keep a record of his living accommodations in the desert. He took black-and-white photos of his tent and vehicle in different locations in North Africa. He likely wanted to show the rocky area and greenery in this color photo, which would appear better in color than in a muted black-and-white image.

A hillside fortification overlooks plateaus in the desert.

Netting and sandbags cover a makeshift rocky crawl space from in which a gunner could hide. Rommel seems to have crouched to the side so his camera could show the turret's view towards enemy lines. The variations of beige and bleached landscape under intense sun and heat undoubtedly presented challenges for sentries posted there.

Rommel's Italian troops wear winter coats as they sit behind a gun, whose barrel points out from desert brush and sandbags.

The serious looks on the most of the soldiers' faces indicate this was a candid image rather than a staged one. Rommel took many ordinary photos of his troops. He liked to capture greenery in his photographs of landscapes in Europe. Perhaps in the desert, he also wanted to capture the greenery of the desert shrubs and uniforms in this color photo.

Soldiers gather around artillery as dust clouds rise from the ground next to the wheels.

The blur of this image indicates the gun fired seconds before Rommel snapped the photo. Some soldiers have their hands raised up to their chins and faces, perhaps to protect their faces from flying dust. One man near the gun barrel covers his ears. Rommel also snapped other battlefront images in black-and-white of artillery being fired.

The silhouette of a tank sits in the middle of the horizon as smoke plumes curl in the sky from burning vehicles on each side.

Rommel photographed a battle as it unfolded in the distance. Sand shields the wheels of speeding vehicles in several locations on the horizon as burning smoke indicates successful strikes against some tanks.

A young German soldier pauses next to artillery that is draped by a canvas.

The soldier, who occupies the center of the frame, is the focal point of this image rather than the gun.

Two Italian soldiers are involved in some activity next to a gun surrounded by boxes of ammunition.

The angle of the image indicates Rommel stood on a low wall made of rocks, visible behind the men, when taking this candid photo of his troops at work.

8. 9. 1915
Ansicht von Norden

Rommel and his fellow infantrymen launch a surprise attack through a smokescreen during a trench battle in the Argonnes in September 1915, causing French soldiers to surrender.

This illustration resembles many photos Rommel took during the heat of battle. His WWII pictures of the German invasion of France also include many photos of French soldiers with their hands raised in surrender, as in this drawing.

• • •

"It is of the utmost importance to the commander to have a good knowledge of the battlefield and of his own and his enemy's positions on the ground. It is often not a question of which of the opposing commanders is mentally higher qualified, or which has the greater experience, but which of them has the better grasp of the battlefield."

—Rommel

3

Across Borders

Rommel appears to have taken this closeup photo of the remnants of a building as he flew past in an airplane.

Crumbling walls of a building left in ruins in the desert.

Rommel enjoyed traveling and visiting diverse places. His writings indicate he was curious about different people and countries. His wife, Lucie, was Polish and Italian, and spoke different languages including French. Rommel once took her on a cross-country motorcycle trip from Germany through Italy during the interwar years.

He was interested in interacting with ordinary people and seeing their customs firsthand. He wrote about his experiences with people of France, Italy, North Africa, San Marino, and Denmark, in addition to the British, Australian and Indian troops he encountered in North Africa. He took many pictures of people and places.

Unlike other German officers, Rommel had limited enthusiasm for culture expressed through fine arts. In an era when the Third Reich promoted neoclassicism and Wagnerian operas, Rommel limited his artistic interests to photography, drawing and stamp-collecting. He was blasé during a tour of the Vatican, much to his wife's dismay, and ridiculed fellow officers in Africa for collecting ancient Roman pottery shards. However he recognized the value of fine art on some level — he photographed architecture, and once saved a medieval tapestry from an Allied bombing raid at La Roche Guyon in 1944.

Like most German soldiers, Rommel knew very little about North Africa before he arrived there. His letters reveal he was excited to travel to a new continent. In a 1941 photograph, Rommel appears standing in the desert holding a book called, *"Unvergessenes Kamerun: Zehn Jahre Wanderungen und Jagden 1928 – 1938."* Penned by German explorer Ernst A. Zwilling, the book's tales of a 10-year trek among wild animals and dense jungles in the Congo likely filled Rommel's imagination with images resembling 1930s Tarzan films. If he intended the book to prepare him for life in North Africa, it was likely a disappointing read.

Both Rommel and his army arrived in Africa wearing safari helmets. These were quickly abandoned after several months due to inefficiency in combat.

Rommel also had romanticized impressions of the Arab world. According to his writings, he was thrilled to meet Bedouin tribesmen, and also expressed disappointment when a place with an exotic Arabic name, Ras el Ali, turned out to be a dingy desert outpost.

Although North Africa turned out different than what he expected, Rommel liked the place. He described in letters how much he admired the beauty of the landscape and said it would be ideal country to explore in peacetime.

A herd of camels grazes in the desert.

The elements of this photo (the sky, hills, camels, and grass) are balanced in harmony, with the sky in the background and vegetation in the foreground in near equal halves of the frame. The faint tire tracks in the grass provide a characteristic curving line that Rommel often places in the center of his composition.

German soldiers stand beside the *Arco de Fileni* monument in Libya. Designed by Italian architect Florestano Di Fausto, the arch contained bronze statues of two legendary men buried alive near the site in ancient times. The arch, a symbol of Italian Libya, was destroyed by Muammar Gaddafi in 1973.

Rommel has positioned the arch directly in the center with the road slightly curving through it. The men on the right side become smaller in the distance as they intersect with the horizon. Hallmarks of his photography are curving lines, objects disappearing into infinity, and bold symmetry.

Flat blue waters in the sea contrast bumpy texture of the sandy beaches.

The sky in both images occupies nearly half of the top frame in balanced proportions with the water and sand. Rommel's use of diagonal planes where the waters meet the shorelines is also evident in the photos.

Defense artillery (far right) line the Mediterranean coast in North Africa.

The calm waters, empty beach, and flowing curvilinear shoreline create a serene natural beauty that stands in stark contrast to the machinery waiting menacingly in the distance on the right. Rommel easily could have focused the photo with the machinery in the center of the frame and ignored the tranquility of this beach scene. Instead, he filled the frame with the landscape and balanced the image with the water on the left and sand on the right. A central focal point is a curving line vanishing as it meets the horizon. The artillery seems to be an aside in this photo.

Vessels wait in a harbor.

Rommel apparently took this photo from a building given the height of the view. The picture could have been taken from a floor overlooking the port or a rooftop. It is composed of multiple layers of lines. The line of the horizon rises above a row of ships in the water. Palm trees form another horizontal line as does the walkway of the street below. A wall of a building, starting at an angle in the center of the frame, juts to the right of the image, dominating the other lines in the photo.

• • •

"Tobruk was one of the strongest fortresses in North Africa. In 1941, with magnificent troops in its garrison, it had presented us with immense difficulties. Many attacks had collapsed in its defenses and much of its outer perimeter had literally been soaked in blood. Often the battle had raged around a square yard at a time."

—**Rommel**

A mosque in the distance.

Rommel took this photo at an angle showing the terrain rising toward the mosque. The mosque is almost perfectly aligned in the center, providing balance and symmetry.

A German soldier (right) stands near an ancient desert fortress in North Africa.

A group of men stand under vine-covered trees in the desert.

• • •

(Rommel's letter to his wife, Lucie)

• March 26, 1941 •

"Yesterday an Italian General...made me a present of a *burnouse* (Arab hooded cloak). It's a magnificent thing — blue-black with red silk and embroidery. It would do well for you as a theater cloak."

• • •

"On September 21, I flew with Gause and Bayerlein to inspect the German-Italian garrison at the Siwa oasis, where we were given an enthusiastic welcome by the Arab population. We presented gifts to the local chiefs and photographed the tribesmen in their magnificent colored robes. I was presented with an envelope on which was stuck every postage stamp issued in the oasis, stamped with that day's postmark."

—Rommel

Two photos of a man dressed in Bedouin attire.

A map of Europe sketched by Rommel illustrates the battles he fought in as an infantryman during WWI.

Rommel liked geography. He drew hundreds of maps for his book "Infantry Attacks." Maps combined his love of adventure, drawing, and mathematics. Rommel was an avid stamp collector, which also appealed to his interests in geography, travel, and artistic imagery.

4

In the Countryside

Rommel's Chief of Staff, Alfred Gause, sits on rocks surrounded by yellow wildflowers in North Africa.

Rommel was an avid outdoors man. He enjoyed being physically active and in nature; he loved skiing, hunting, fishing, swimming, horseback riding, hiking and other athletic pursuits. His wife often accompanied him in these pastimes. His family, friends and fellow soldiers said Rommel's idea of a good day was one spent outside.

Affinity with nature and outdoor activities are an inherent part of German culture. The German language has special and unique words to denote outdoor behaviors, which do not exist in other languages like English. For example, the word *spazieren*, meaning "to go walking outside," is different from the word used for normal walking and has a freer tone to it. The German word *wandern* can mean both "to hike" or "to roam," combining the concept of wilderness and exploration.

Like many Germans, Rommel also felt stirred by the sight of flowers and natural beauty, which is evidenced by his writings and many photographs of these subjects. Due to modern stereotypes, Germans are not generally viewed by others as poetic or sentimental—however, the opposite is true. Nature especially has emotional significance for Germans.

Over many centuries, German writers, poets, composers and philosophers have produced an abundance of extremely vivid verses, songs and literature. A majority of these expressions combine human emotion with features of nature such as trees, weather, rivers, forests, birds, or flowers. Generally speaking, the presence or absence of natural beauty affects or underscores the tone of the writings or lyrics.

A field of wildflowers in North Africa.

In this photo series, Rommel has stopped momentarily during his travels in the countryside to take photos of brilliant yellow wildflowers. He appears to have been struck by their natural beauty within the landscape, even to the point of having a fellow soldier leave a vehicle to pose for a photo.

Rommel also emphasizes nature in his writings from both WWI and WWII. Both his black-and-white and color photos contain various types of landscapes and natural features.

• • •

(Rommel's letter to his wife)
• March 3, 1943 •

"It's spring outside, blossoming trees and meadows, sunshine. The world could be so beautiful for all men. Such infinite possibilities exist to make them contented and happy. There is so much that could be done—especially here in Africa with its wide-open spaces."

A photo series with three different views of the wildflowers.

It is obvious from these photos that Rommel walked around in the field taking a variety of different views of the flowers. The photo above is a closeup of the delicate flower blooms.

The photos on the right show the flowers from various vantage points. The picture on the lower right was taken of the field from a higher angle, possibly while Rommel was in his car.

The image on the upper right looks as if it was taken when he stood among the flowers in the field. The blooms in the foreground dominate the composition of the picture, while the sky forms a narrow blue line across the top.

In general, Rommel's landscape pictures depict elements balanced in equal proportion to each other (in equal parts in the foreground, middle ground, and background). However, in this series, the flowers fill the frames with their brilliant yellow blooms.

Photos of wildflowers taken by Rommel as his vehicle travels behind two
other German vehicles.

By the appearance of the flower patches, it appears the photo on top was taken prior
to the lower one as Rommel traveled through and around the field in a convoy.

Aerial photos of a forest (date and location unknown).

These images were taken in Europe. They look similar to black and white photos he took while reconnoitering German troop movements in France.

Trees dot the barren landscape.

Rommel took this photo from the vantage point of a plane he was traveling in. The irregular lines of trees in the center of the image create an interesting linear focal point in the photo.

This image is blurry and therefore an unusual find among Rommel's personal photo collection, since most of his shots are in focus. Despite its quality, this picture is included in this book because it is interesting that one of history's toughest generals and most talented military strategists took time to capture an image of delicate flowers and keep it with his treasured photo remembrances.

Sprigs of white flowers.

An unidentified woman, possibly Rommel's sister Helene, sits near wildflowers by a lake.

Trees cast reflections in the peaceful water of a lake in a forest.

This photo shows Rommel's characteristic curvilinear pattern with the shoreline.

Rommel's wife, Lucie, stands on the second floor of a home looking at Rommel as he takes her photo.

The sideways vantage point of the photo highlights the intricate woodwork of the building, creating texture and lines. Lucie appears in the direct center as the focal point, but is overshadowed by the architecture set against a backdrop of trees. Rommel's photo collection, particularly his black-and-white images, demonstrate his interest in nature photos, particularly trees. This photo would seem to contain many items of interest to Rommel as a photographer: natural beauty, his family, and geometric patterns in his surroundings.

• • •

(Rommel's letter to his wife)
• Jan. 23, 1943 •
"There is lovely country around here, one would like to travel through it at ease in peacetime. Will that ever be?"

A closeup of Lucie from the photo above.

A French command post in the Argonne Forest in 1915.

Rommel's illustration above details linear geometric shapes of wooden architecture near trees, as in his photo on the opposite page.

• • •

(Rommel's letter to his wife during retreat)
• Dec. 16, 1942 •

"We've made camp in flower-decked meadows. But we're on the way back...there's no prospect of the situation improving. Eight more days to Christmas. I wonder where we'll be then."

5

In the Street

An Italian soldier (left) looks at Rommel who is photographing Arab men shining shoes.

Rommel's photography indicates he liked to go exploring in local streets when he had the opportunity in order to document life around him. His black-and-white photos from France and other locations show his interest in architecture, vehicles, and unusual or visually interesting scenes.

His collection contains no staged or exaggerated photos. He seemed to wish to take candid photos of people and their environments.

It is interesting to note that, while Rommel photographed most of his European street scenes in black-and-white, his North African street scenes are all in color with almost no black-and-white versions. Rommel had never visited the African continent or the Middle East prior to WWII. It appears he was so impressed by his new surroundings—so very different from anything he had seen before in Europe—that he chose to document North African street scenes exclusively with color film.

There are also relatively fewer North African street scenes in Rommel's collection than those he took in Europe. This is likely due to the fact that Rommel was rarely able to visit cities in North Africa. He spent most of his time traveling through desert wildernesses, occasionally passing through tiny villages or forsaken outposts. He often toured the frontlines during his spare time and never stayed in one place for very long, due to both military actions and assassination attempts.

When German troops arrived in North Africa in 1941, they were reviewed by Rommel and Italian commanders and processed through the crowded streets of Tripoli, Libya, with many civilian spectators.

An Arab man adjusts a mule cart.

The man is the central element while the mule on the right and road on the left are of lesser importance. It is interesting that Rommel chose to frame the left side of this image with the street becoming more obscure as it disappears into the horizon. Rommel could have stood closer to the man for a closeup without choosing to show the street.

• • •

"Driving along the road...we passed long columns of Arabs driving pack animals laden with loot. They were carrying away everything movable that could be stripped...The Americans had blown up their ammunition in the citadel without any warning to the people living in the neighborhood and 30 houses had collapsed...The people were consequently very bitter towards the Americans and were noisily celebrating their liberation."

—Rommel, 1943

A group of boys walk along a street in North Africa.

This photo features one of Rommel's favorite composition techniques: a prominent central road with subjects that gradually disappear into infinity. The boy on the far right looks directly at the camera as the lens captures the moment. Two other boys in the group also appear aware that their photo is being taken. In the middle of the frame, slightly to the left, a small boy looks down at the street. He doesn't seem to notice a group of Italian soldiers nearby. Standing next to the open door in the middle of the frame, a couple of Italian soldiers watch Rommel take the photo. The soldier nearest to the door turns his head to look over his shoulder at the photographer.

• • •

"It made one's hair stand on end to see the sort of equipment with which the Duce (Mussolini) had sent his troops into battle."

—Rommel

A man walks past an outdoor area in North Africa.

Both men in the photo are framed by palm trees. The man in the overcoat (left) looks away from the camera through an open archway. The man in the foreground (right) is walking towards a palm tree, whose leaves fold over into the frame of the photo. A fountain with Arabic writing occupies the center middle ground, while chairs facing different directions are scattered nearby. It appears Rommel took a closeup of a street scene as a memento for his personal photo collection.

• • •

"During January, a number of our A.A. gunners succeeded in surprising a British column...and captured the commander of the 1st S.A.S. Regiment, Lt. Col. David Stirling...He managed to escape and made his way to some Arabs, to whom he offered a reward to return him to British lines. But his bid must have been too small, for the Arabs, with their usual eye for business, offered him to us for 11 pounds of tea—a bargain which we soon clinched."

—Rommel

Two soldiers walk alongside a man in a street in North Africa.

This photo is vertically balanced, which is unusual in Rommel's work. The open street scene on the right is contrasted by the closed door and building on the left. Both sides of the photo are divided in nearly equal proportion. A group of boys stand along the sidewalk in the center of the frame, while the curving street disappears from view.

• • •

"The men received their tropical kit early next morning, and by 11 o'clock were fallen in on the square in front of Government House. They radiated complete assurance of victory, and the change of atmosphere did not pass unnoticed in Tripoli."

—Rommel

Italienischer Nachtangriff

Italian troops swept through village streets and attacked Rommel and his troops head-on in a fierce night attack during the Battle at Longarone in 1917.

As with many of Rommel's photos, this illustration of a European village features a dramatically curving road combined with his stylized use of shadows to dramatize the image.

• • •

Venturing into urban areas was not always safe for German soldiers during wartime. Battlefields were not the only places where mortal danger lurked, according to this account by Rommel of an experience in France 1940.

"In the western outskirts of Flers we passed a large square crowded, as usual, with French soldiers and civilians. Suddenly a civilian a few yards from the column ran towards my car with drawn revolver, intending to shoot, but French troops pulled him up short and prevented him carrying out his purpose. We drove on."

—Rommel

6

By the Sea

A German soldier, likely Rommel's driver, stands near a car and a truck. The noses of both vehicles point toward a pair of ships in the harbor. Rommel stood directly aligned with an opening between both vehicles to balance the machines in symmetry with the vessels in the water.

The sea was significant to Rommel for several different reasons. In North Africa, the Mediterranean Sea was one of the only avenues of transport for supplies sent from Europe to his troops, including ammunition, weapons, and gasoline. Being a hands-on leader, Rommel often watched supplies being unloaded at dock. Combated by the Luftwaffe and the Italian Navy, the British Royal Navy and Air Force often bombed and sank German supply ships. The German High Command lacked a vested interest in Rommel's Afrika Korps and, instead, focused on propaganda efforts on the Eastern Front, which led to a cease of regular supplies sent to Africa. Rommel attributed the eventual defeat of his army in Africa to shortages of and failure to receive much-needed supplies.

The sea was also important to Rommel as a desert soldier. Water was a rare commodity in the North African wilderness. The intense heat and endless dust made it easy for both

Allied and German soldiers to become dirty and soaked with perspiration. They often resorted to washing their sweat-soaked clothes with sand; otherwise, the uniforms would become too stiff and grimy to wear. Soldiers rarely had chances to bathe and developed skin sores. Dirty water was filtered and hoarded. Rommel was also in the same situation—washing his clothes, bathing, and even removing his boots were noted in his letters as rare and happy occasions. The sea provided Rommel and other German soldiers with an opportunity to wash and clean themselves and their clothing.

It is likely Rommel also appreciated the ocean for cultural reasons. Germans tend to view going to the beach as a rare treat. Germany has only one coastline that lies in the far north, in immediate proximity to Scandinavia. A trip to the beach for many Germans—particularly Southern Germans like Rommel—involves packing, travel and competition with other beachgoers for room along a crowded shoreline. The North Sea is not known for being very warm or sunny, either. Germans often vacation to foreign countries to enjoy the phenomenon of sunlit beaches.

While many of Rommel's black-and-white photos of the Mediterranean emphasize fortifications and military-related actions, his color photography focuses on blue ocean water, docked ships, and sandy beaches.

• • •

(Rommel's letter to his wife)
• March 26, 1941 •

"Spent our first day by the sea. It's a very lovely place and it's as good as being in a hotel in my comfortable caravan. Bathe in the sea in the mornings, it's already beautifully warm."

German soldiers wait as cargo is being unloaded at a port in North Africa.

Rommel works to gain alternate views of his subjects in these photos. Framed by men on both sides, the water and distant vista takes center stage in the top image. In the lower photo, Rommel has stepped away from the soldiers to stand behind the trio of men. The frame expands so the shirtless man is in the center, while a new view of a vessel appears on the left as another man passes by in the middle ground.

Black smoke emits from an approaching vessel (left) in the port.

The metal rails at the forefront of the photo depict intersecting diagonal lines in the composition.

A fishing boat flanks a ship in port.

The pavement (left) forms a diagonal pattern as the ship dominates the center.

A bent tree stands alongside a port in North Africa.

This photo frames two cargo boats (center) in diagonal contrast with silver submarines. The jetty in the middle ground forms one linear shape while the concrete shoreline (left) takes on a zigzag shape. The dark band at the top left of the photo suggests Rommel took this photo from inside a vehicle as he drove past.

A fishing boat sails past two small vessels that float next to a large ship. A German flag flutters from on vessel (center).

Apparently working at the docks, the shirtless German men on the boats appear to look at Rommel as he takes the photo.

Boats clutter an inlet in a port.

The water forms a thin slice of blue in the center of the frame in this balanced image.

A jetty divides vessels in a port.

The blue sky and sea are balanced in almost equal measure. A jetty occupies the center of the image almost at the point of the horizon. The vantage point of this photo could indicate it was taken while Rommel was on a boat in the harbor.

Trucks (right) travel to meet the ships in the harbor.

The circular road frames this image with a curving line, which Rommel uses in many of his compositions. The trucks also decrease in size as they drive off into the distance.

A lone barrel (right) lays in front of netting while dockyard workers in the distance prepare to unload cargo.

The prominent cylindrical shapes appear to have caught Rommel's eye in this photo.

White buildings gleam in the background above a row of ships moored in an inlet.

The hills, buildings, vessels, water, land, and discolored soil form stacks of horizontal layers, adding dimension to this photo. Rommel could have stepped over the darker strip of soil that cuts through the foreground for a closer view of the ships, but chose to include this stripe as an important element in the composition of this picture.

Four men in a rowboat turn their attention to something out of view.

A corner of sidewalk (lower left) indicates Rommel was standing at the water's edge while he took this photo, which features the men in the rowboat as a focal point.

A lone German soldier stands in the center of a busy dockyard.

A crane
hovers
in the
sky while
German
soldiers
mingle
near a
loading
area.

Rommel took both images with the cranes on the same side of the port. He was likely overseeing activities. His black-and-white photos feature machinery. His personal interests included machinery and how different technology worked.

Men crowd around wooden crates of cargo on a pier next to a vessel.

Rommel is known for his camaraderie with his troops. The men on the pier are the main focus of this photo. The men are dressed in a variety of outfits. Most are in uniform. Some wear pith helmets while others have caps. Some soldiers are in shorts and some wear pants. Some soldiers are on land while others are on the vessel. Interspersed in the crowd are North African dockyard workers.

• • •

(Rommel's letter to his wife)
• June 26, 1942 •

"For days now I've been camping out in the car...I've had my headquarters by the sea for the past 20 hours and bathed yesterday and today. But the water doesn't refresh, it's much too hot."

Two sailors (center, right) walk near German soldiers on a pier.

The partial appearance of a German soldier (left) in the image indicates Rommel was standing at a high vantage point when he took this closeup photo of work at the dock.

German and Italian soldiers stand on a dock.

A German soldier leaning on a wooden crate is in the center of the frame. A "No Smoking" sign in German hangs from a smokestack above the men. Crates are shown on the dock and loaded onto a truck (left). Gas cans are visible next to metal drums.

German soldiers walk in a line atop a boat loaded with cargo in North Africa.

This photo contains an interesting interplay between light and darkness. The men under the bright gaze of the sun on the vessel's surface are contrasted with the immense shadows below in the ship's cargo hold. The rooftop surface of the vessel occupies nearly half the frame in an equal part with the gaping opening below.

Rommel's photos often depict multiple parallel and intersecting curved lines. This photo is no exception. The line of men, who all seem to be staring into the camera, curve to the right side of this photo. They stand on a rooftop that has bending lines underneath their feet. Another pair of slanting lines is formed by the sides of this ship.

His photo collection contains black-and-white images of the interior of a cargo ship being unloaded.

A night roadblock bars the path of Rommel and his troops near Longarone in
1917. Accidental noise drew the attention of enemy machine guns, which began
firing straight at the Germans from behind the barrier. "Machine gun fire at
80 yards, without the chance to take cover, is enough to make you lose your
mind," Rommel wrote in *"Infantry Attacks,"* while discussing this experience.
"Death stands very close to a person in such circumstances."

In this sketch, Rommel uses the same visual technique that can be seen in many of
his seaside images. He uses objects and variations in the landscape and scenery to create
strong diagonal and horizontal lines that divide the frame.

7

In the Desert

The tops of trees dot ravines within a craggy hill in the desert.

Rommel visited diverse desert terrains during his time in North Africa. He spent much time in Libya and Tunisia. In addition to sandstorms, dryness and smothering heat, he experienced cold and rainy seasons, saw flowery green expanses in the wilderness, and fought in steep terrain in 1943 which he compared to Alpine slopes.

He adapted well to desert warfare—the vast expanses of wasteland allowed him and his troops to be mobile and ingenious, appearing and disappearing from various places and using illusions to their advantage.

The desert was also a place of hardship. Extreme temperatures, lack of water, dirty sand, insects, rocky terrain and colossal storms made life grim for soldiers. Many of Rommel's staff officers and subordinates fell sick and had to be given leave to recover.

Rommel had a tough constitution and lasted longer without significant problems than men half his age. Nevertheless, he experienced health problems that eventually forced him to take a brief leave for his recovery. He caught a severe case of bacterial diphtheria, likely due to contaminated water, and developed sepsis—dangerously low blood pressure. To this was added extreme stress due to battle situations. Rommel started to have blackouts on the

The bright floral colors brighten an otherwise bleak desert color scheme. A light tank (center) appears to be hidden in the trees.

The blooms of maroon flowers rise from desolate rocky terrain.

battlefield and had difficulty breathing. His worsening condition worried his staff officers. He resisted taking sick leave, but was ordered to do so. Rommel agreed on the condition that he could reassume command after he recovered.

Rommel's brief sojourn at a mountain resort in Austria did not last long—the temporary commander died of a heart attack shortly after arriving on the frontlines. Rommel wrote that he could not take his mind off events in Africa and was glad to take charge of the troops again.

Nevertheless, Rommel wrote to his wife that he found it difficult to readjust to the harshness of desert life after his brief stay at home with his family. In the months that followed, he frequently wrote about missing home and expressed worries about the end of the war. He also noted that it was easy to lose track of time in the desert, and was at times unable to date his letters.

● ● ●

(Rommel's letter to his wife)
• April 8, 1941 •
"We've been attacking for days now in the endless desert and have
lost all idea of space and time...Our main force is on its way up after a
220-mile march over the sand and rock of the desert."

The slope of a stone plateau descends gracefully before a sweeping desert vista.

White flowers bloom on a desert hillside in North Africa.

Multiple diagonal lines are formed throughout this photo in the slopes of the terrain and roadways.

Geologic strata are revealed in an aerial view of a desert mountain.

The narrow valley below forms a curving central focal point in this rugged image taken as Rommel flew past in his airplane.

A clearing forms a level path at the base of desert hillsides.

Rommel composed this image so that the valley forms a prominent diagonal middle stripe separating the rocky hills in the foreground and background.

A valley sits between rocky terrain in North Africa.

Rommel's interest in curvilinear shapes is shown in this photo. A vertical asymmetrical crevice divides this image from the top to the bottom of the frame.

Green desert terrain is visible from the window of Rommel's aircraft.

With part of the airplane visible in these photos, it is easy to imagine Rommel seated inside the aircraft when he captured these shots. Also of interest is the low altitude at which he was flying when this photo (above) was taken.

Two views of what appear to be bends in the same dry riverbed in North Africa.

A volcanic formation (right) rises in the distance from gravel plains in North Africa.

Rommel created an interesting image by placing the volcanic formation on the right side. The right focal point highlights the vast immensity of the desert, which was so different from luxuriant green German landscapes. His composition is nearly a perfect balance in equal parts between the sky and the land below.

An aerial view of plateau formations in the desert.

A wide diagonal path across opposite corners of the frame is created in the way Rommel positions the land formations.

A mosque and several buildings stand outside an oasis.

Sand glistens under the harsh sun in North Africa.

The earth rises to extreme heights in an aerial view of a sandstorm.

Rommel undoubtedly captured this image of the sandstorm for personal rather than military use. His plane, visible in the right corner, was flying at a low altitude, making it likely that he experienced some turbulence from the powerful winds in this sandstorm.

Another aerial view of a sandstorm.

The terrain in this photo looks different from the one above. Rommel takes this image with the foreground, middle ground, and background at diagonal planes that seem to form layers stacked. The angle of this photo and tire tracks in the dirt (lower left) indicate Rommel's photo was taken as his plane was either landing or taking off.

Various angles of rocky cliffs appear to have been taken in the same place in North Africa.

German soldiers look over the ledge of a stone plateau in North Africa.

Rommel contrasts the enormity of the cliff against the small stature of the men, who stand above it its edge. In the far distance, a Panzer overlooks the desert plains below.

A closeup of the edge of the cliff shown above.

German infantrymen rush through trenches amid explosions during WWI.

Like Rommel's photos taken in the heat of battle, this illustration has a strong focal point of soldiers in action. He also regularly composed images this way when photographing soldiers in trenches in North Africa. In those images, he adopted a viewpoint of looking slightly over soldiers (rather than at an eye-level perspective) who are shown in curving rows that cut through the center of a picture .

8

In the Air

Rommel sits in the cockpit of Junkers Ju 87 Stuka dive bomber in North Africa.

Rommel was an intrepid pilot. He had an interest in aviation since his youth. At age 14, he built—and crashed—a full-scale glider with friends. He continued to pursue his interest in flying during WWII and used his mechanical skills to learn how to fly his own plane. He was comfortable in the air and enjoyed going on reconnaissance missions. He was also known to use his plane to make sudden appearances among his men in unexpected locations. German troops were encouraged by the sight of Rommel's plane and enjoyed waving at him from the ground as he passed overhead.

While flying, Rommel took many photographs. Photos were intended for military reconnaissance, battle maps and plans, or simply for his own personal interest.

Rommel's daring airplane exploits often placed him in harrowing situations. Once, he nearly landed on a British airstrip and made a narrow escape amid gunfire. He was nearly shot down by his own Italian troops, who failed to recognize a German plane. Another time, he crashed into a sand bank while landing and was stranded with a marooned German soldier as a convoy of British vehicles charged toward them—he and the soldier tried to defend themselves with a machine gun, and discovered the firing pin was missing. They barely escaped after finding a truck in the area.

These color photos show Rommel's interest in natural scenery, military formations, and strategic regions.

A closeup of Rommel from the photo above.

Dust clouds rise from a Panzer as it speeds past an empty German plane in North Africa.

This plane is likely Rommel's Fieseler Storch aircraft, which he used frequently for reconnaissance. Wing beams from it are visible in many of Rommel's photos. The wings of the plane cast a long shadow across the center of the image and form a dominant line on the ground below the horizon. Rommel could have taken the photo with the plane positioned in the middle, but he aimed his lens to place the airplane off center, which causes shadows to create a dramatic effect.

• • •

"Through my daily flights between Tripoli and the front, I came to know Tripolitania very well from the air and formed a great admiration for the colonizing achievement of the Italians."

—Rommel

A long road sweeps past a cluster of white buildings in North Africa.

Rommel's air reconnaissance for his military operations was an important part of his battle strategy.

Rommel's finger inadvertently appears in the photo of a desert community.

Men and supply trucks are busy in what appears to be a German depot.

Clearings in the trees reveal two buildings next to a tilled field.

Green plateaus cascade into plains in North Africa.

The wing and body of Rommel's aircraft can be seen in the frame of this photo.

An oasis is the site of heavy traffic shown by the tire tracks in the surrounding dirt.

Rommel composed this photo with the zigzag irrigation ditch in the center of the frame, providing a balanced view of both sides of the desert.

A convoy of vehicles crosses a bridge in North Africa.

The wing tip of Rommel's plane, flying at a low altitude, can be seen (right). The dry riverbed curves across the frame before disappearing from view.

A roadway loops up a steep plateau.

Rommel's aerial reconnaissance photos in North Africa demonstrate his interest in surrounding infrastructure. Both photos depict strong diagonal elements in his compositions.

Rommel watches from above as a line of tanks roar across the sand in his direction.

Rommel's airplane is flying alongside tanks leaving plumes of sand as they race across the desert to battle.

Rommel flies at low altitude alongside a group of soldiers in jeeps traveling through the desert.

There are numerous tire tracks in the sand at the bottom of this photo, which indicate this location was a high traffic area. This series of photos reveals that Rommel used his plane to monitor troop movements. His black-and-white photos show he took many pictures of battles unfolding while monitoring developments from his airplane above.

• • •

"Mobile warfare in the desert has often and rightly been compared with a battle at sea—where it is equally wrong to attack piecemeal and leave half the fleet in port during battle."

—Rommel

While this image is slightly blurry, it shows soldiers looking up at Rommel as he flew past.

Also slightly out of focus, this photo was taken of German troops approaching.
This photo is interesting since the dust in the image was likely produced when Rommel's airplane was either taking off from or landing on a desert airstrip.

A makeshift German airfield in a grassy area near a town.

A more distant view of the German airfield.

These photos may have been taken by Rommel when he was in the cockpit of the Stuka dive bomber plane previously shown.

Rommel, piloting what seems to be a Stuka dive bomber, approaches salt marshes in Africa.

This photo is one of abstract shapes. Rommel uses the airplane wing as one of his characteristic diagonal elements to divide this image nearly in half in a neat balance.

Rommel's airplane reconnaissance enabled him to perceive things that his troops on the ground could not, as in this instance in North Africa in 1941:

"After taking off (in my plane) again I discovered several columns of German and Italian tanks...I landed and reprimanded them for being so slow. Apparently the leading vehicles, while crossing a dried-out salt marsh, had seen what appeared to be a wide stretch of water away to the east and turned back. It was, of course, only a mirage—a common enough occurrence in that district. I now ordered them to press on forward as fast as they could."

—Rommel

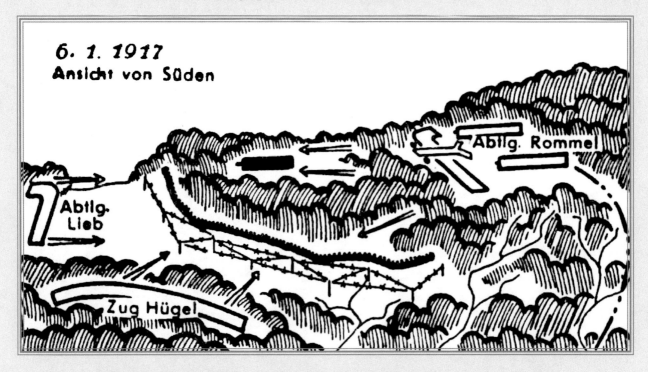

Rommel's sketch details a battle that unfolded in Romania on Jan. 6, 1917.

Like his aerial photos, this sketch contains many layered details and different textures. Many of Rommel's aerial photos were intended for the same purpose as this drawing: to allow him to make accurate battle plans based on terrain, and to create clear pictures of his military actions. In some of his WWII photos that he intended to publish in a military textbook, Rommel penciled notes and diagrams on the photographs similar to those in this sketch.

9

With the Men

A German soldier stands guard in North Africa

Rommel began his Army career as an enlisted man and paid his own way through officer cadet school. As a soldier, he had a different perspective than other members of the German military, who often came from aristocratic families.

Rommel's experiences as an infantryman in WWI left lasting impressions on him. As a foot soldier, armed with a rifle and bayonet, he charged across trenches, scaled mountainsides and engaged in fierce gunfights with the peril of death constantly near. He and his fellows were often left starving with no protection from bombs. Rommel was wounded three times in action—one severe leg injury nearly crippled him and required him to walk with a cane for some time afterward. He saw many of his comrades die in action and witnessed soldiers make great personal sacrifices, which he memorialized in *"Infantry Attacks."*

According to his wife, Rommel was quiet about his WWI experiences and rarely discussed them at home. He formed close bonds with his comrades which remained throughout his life. During the severe financial depression and poverty that struck Germany after WWI, Rommel formed a group called the "Old Comrades Association"

A structure has been camouflaged along the sandy roadside.

to financially support other veterans he served with. He remained active in this group until his death in 1944.

Rommel had a close personal attachment to his men and considered them comrades rather than subordinates. He often wrote about his sense of responsibility to them and his gratitude for their trust in him.

His men had both a high admiration and affection for him. Rommel enjoyed spending time among the ranks. He liked talk with the men, joke with them and share food. He also fought at the frontlines among them and worked alongside them—once he assisted soldiers to clear mines from an area. His soldiers were devoted to him. They viewed Rommel both a commander and a brother-in-arms, and were often inspired to make great efforts on the battlefield because of him. They also guarded him without his knowledge.

After being summoned to Europe for a military briefing, Rommel expected to return to North Africa to resume command of his men. Instead, he was sent to Austria and removed of his post. His ultimate separation from the men in Africa, followed by their surrender, was both a shock and a tremendous blow to him. He wrote to his wife that it "left a bad scar."

He attempted to keep in touch with his soldiers who became POWs in the U.S., New Zealand and Canada. His writings about the Afrika Korps defeat and surrender contain scathing criticism of German military leadership and bitter regrets.

For many years after Rommel's death, former Afrika Korps soldiers visited his grave annually and conducted a memorial service in his honor.

Soldiers stand next to a jeep and small tent marked with a Red Cross (right), while a camouflaged tent stands on the opposite side in the desert.

Rommel's photo evokes a sense of desolation in the desert as brush, tents, men, and vehicles are the only objects rising from the vast expanse of barren soil. Medical treatment there was very difficult for the sick and wounded.

A German and Italian soldier watch Rommel take their photo, while other soldiers hide supplies in a dugout.

Italian soldiers rest in groups as their rifles stand next to covered supplies.

Instead of focusing a single group of soldiers, Rommel composes this image with an interesting array of clusters of men. In the center of the frame, a tiny group appears on the horizon. Starting from that central point, each group becomes more visible as they become closer to the photographer.

German soldiers with shovels walk near a covered mound, while others stand at a nearby tent.

In the distance on the right, an airplane is parked in the grassy field.

German and Italian soldiers gather at the back of a truck.

A soldier in the driver's seat of a convoy vehicle turns his head while being photographed.

A lean-to tent is attached to the supply truck. Branches cover the tarp on a truck parked alongside. The camouflage indicates that the goods transported needed to be hidden.

A German soldier on a hill stands near a gun battery as other soldiers dig a trench in the sand below.

Rommel's compositions in his photos often have curvilinear elements and this image is no exception. The tire tracks at the forefront of the picture swerve off from sight in the middle of the frame. The lone soldier watches from atop a sloping hillside, while the trenches and men inside them form the final diagonal paths.

A soldier leans on a vehicle near two tents that peer from hiding places in the sand.

Rommel carefully balanced the trio of objects in this composition. The top of the tent in the center is flanked in equal measure by the other tent and vehicle. By positioning his lens with large sand before and after the focal points, he captures the enormity of this lifeless desert vista in contrast to the people.

Rommel, in a pith helmet, smiles next to an unidentified German soldier in their camp.

Despite seeming to be in good spirits, Rommel has dark circles under his eyes. He rarely had chances to rest and was constantly on the move during battle. His sleeping truck is in the background. On page 25, Rommel's sleeper has been painted in camouflage.

• • •

(Rommel's letter to his wife)
• April 10, 1941 •

"After a long desert march I reached the sea the evening before last...I'm well. My caravan arrived at last early this morning and I'm hoping to sleep in it again."

Various military vehicles and soldiers surround this building in the desert.

This outpost is believed to be one of Rommel's headquarters in North Africa.

Men inside a courtyard in a desert.
Rommel was likely contrasting the structure with the remarkable stone hillside.

Two unknown German officers pose for a picture.

Rommel's photo collection contains no propaganda photos and rarely any photos of officers. The majority of soldiers' photos he saved were images of ordinary troops. Although this photo is slightly out of focus, it is included because it must have meant something to Rommel to belong to his personal portfolio of images.

Rommel is unaware this photo is being taken of him shirtless and barefoot,
while German and Italian soldiers surrounding him turn to the camera.

Whoever took this photo gave it to Rommel later because the image found its way into his personal collection. Because of his uncharacteristic appearance in this image, it stands out among his photo collection. It appears that the main intention of the photographer was to capture a casual image of Rommel on film rather than for propaganda purposes.

• • •

(Rommel's letter to his wife)

• July 14, 1942 •

"Physically I'm very well. I'm wearing shorts for the first time today—it's pretty hot."

A closeup of Rommel from
the photo above.

A rock ridge shields a tent and camouflaged supplies from view while men talk in a dirt clearing.

The men in the center are overshadowed by horizontal plateaus cutting through the desert below the horizon.

A tank, surrounded by sandbags, and a tent wait on the ridge of a sandy hillside.

By looking up to the Panzer with its gun barrel outstretched over the hill and centering it in the frame, Rommel creates a dramatic effect in this image.

Rommel meets unidentified local dignitaries in North Africa in September 1942.

These photos were likely taken during the same event described on P. 39. Rommel appears to be holding the envelope with stamps given to him as a gift by the Arabs at the oasis. The man standing behind Rommel wearing a fez is likely an interpreter. They are accompanied by an Italian officer wearing a white dress uniform.

Rommel was very ill at the time these photos were taken and his letters reveal he was in low spirits. This event occurred the day before he surrendered control of the Panzer Army to a temporary replacement. He left for Austria on sick leave, but was recalled to the battlefield shortly afterwards to face defeat at El Alamein.

These images of the formal meeting is the only such event contained in the color photos of his personal collection.

A lone soldier standing at the base of a rocky hill faces the immense desert.

In this powerful photo of a man against the elements, Rommel demonstrates several of his favorite visual techniques. A single figure of a person set against an immense backdrop often appears in his black-and-white photos. Like the rocky hill, strong curving elements also appear in his pictures. Another frequent element is layered horizontal planes. This effect is achieved above with the tire tracks and sea of shifting sand and shadows rising toward the horizon.

Rommel and his men stand facing a mob of charging enemy soldiers during the Battle for Longarone in 1917. Rommel is standing at the far right near the house. The mob began firing at the Germans at 10 yards and trampled many of them. Rommel escaped capture by jumping over a wall. He ran cross-country to warn his other soldiers and took part in a gun battle against the attackers, which lasted the entire night.

• • •

"The higher the rank, the greater the effect of the example. The men tend to feel no kind of contact with a commander who, they know, is sitting somewhere in headquarters. What they want is what might be termed a physical contact with him. In moments of panic, fatigue or disorganization, or when something out of the ordinary has to be demanded from them, the personal example of the commander works wonders, especially if he has had the wit to create some sort of legend around himself."

—Rommel

• • •

References

This book is not an academic work. It had its early origins as my undergraduate Honor's Thesis, but evolved significantly over time. Therefore I find it unnecessary to make a comprehensive list of all materials which contributed to my knowledge about the topics in this book. I conducted years of in-depth research about Rommel and the war in North Africa. My writings and analysis on the subject matter are based on my own expertise. However, there are several important reference sources which I owe credit to. I cite them here as follows:

- *"The Rommel Papers,"* by Erwin Rommel (edited by B.H. Liddell-Hart and translated by Paul Findlay); with excerpts by Manfred Rommel and General Fritz Bayerlein (Da Capo Press: New York), 1953.
This collection of Erwin Rommel's writings and personal letters was published shortly after the Second World War. At the request of the Rommel family, it was edited by British military historian B.H. Liddell-Hart, whose work Rommel admired during his lifetime. Various eyewitnesses contributed to the book, including Manfred Rommel, his mother Lucie, and General Fritz Bayerlein, who had fought alongside Rommel in North Africa.

- *"Infanterie Greift An"* by Erwin Rommel (Ludwig Voggenreiter Verlag: Potsdam), 1938. This early German edition of Erwin Rommel's military textbook was printed in Fraktur script and contains all of Rommel's original sketches based on his experiences in the First World War. In it, Rommel gives detailed descriptions of his military tactics and includes his recollections of his first experiences as a soldier.

- *"Rommel, the Desert Fox,"* by Desmond Young, (Harper & Brothers: New York), 1950. Desmond Young was a British officer captured as a POW by German troops in WWII North Africa. He experienced the desert war firsthand and met Erwin Rommel in person. While gathering material for this book, he personally interviewed Rommel's family members, friends, fellow soldiers and other eyewitnesses, gained access to original documents, and recorded firsthand testimony.

- *"World War Two: The War in the Desert"* by Richard Collier and the editors of Time-Life Books, (Time Life Books: New Jersey), 1977.
This book gives an overview of desert warfare and the general experiences of German and British soldiers in various areas of North Africa during WWII.

About the English Translations of Rommel's Writings:

The excerpts quoted from Rommel's writings included in this book come from *"The Rommel Papers"* and *"Infanterie Greift An."*

Because Findlay's English translations of Rommel's writings in German were made more than 50 years ago, I occasionally substituted some antiquated British words with modern English equivalents.

Since I am fluent in German, I provided my own translations of Rommel's writings in his WWI book.

About the Author: Zita Steele

Zita Steele is a novelist and artist from the Southwestern state of New Mexico. She writes both fiction and nonfiction. She has expertise in criminology, cybercrime, and international relations. She loves foreign languages and cultures. Zita's stories often involve history and international themes. She likes to create characters who must cross cultural divides to understand each other.

She is currently working on the 4th volume of the nonfiction *"Erwin Rommel: Photographer"* series and also on fiction projects.

Photo by Noël Fletcher

Other Books by Zita Steele

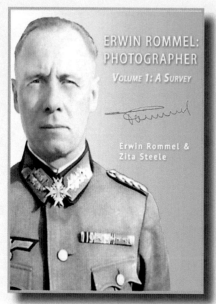

Erwin Rommel Photographer–Vol. 1: A Survey

by ERWIN ROMMEL and ZITA STEELE

Take a journey behind the camera of a world-famous military commander. Experience WWII firsthand from Field Marshal Rommel's private photo collection, seized by U.S. forces in 1945.

View 340+ images, including photos Rommel took during campaigns in France and North Africa and others he collected. Included are Rommel's personal photos of family and friends. The photos are digitally restored for detail. Some are accompanied by Rommel's own handwritten photo captions.

Author/artist Zita Steele uses her knowledge of German language and culture, with in-depth research about Rommel and his campaigns, to provide context for the photos. Zita also analyzes patterns in Rommel's photography to shed a light on the artistic personality of this notable military leader.

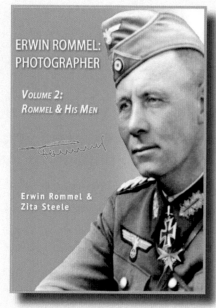

Erwin Rommel Photographer–Vol. 2:

Rommel & His Men

by ERWIN ROMMEL and ZITA STEELE

Take a journey behind the camera of world-famous military commander. Experience life on the frontlines with Field Marshal Erwin Rommel.

View 200+ images from Rommel's private photo collection, seized by U.S. forces in 1945. Join Rommel as he interacts with his German and Italian troops.

See him and his men at work, at rest, and on the move. View Rommel's mementos of his men and military leaders.

This book provides a candid view of Rommel as an ordinary soldier rather than a general. The photos are digitally restored and enhanced for detail. Some are accompanied by Rommel's own handwritten photo captions.

Other Books by Zita Steele

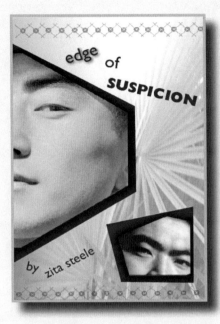

Edge of Suspicion *by* ZITA STEELE

Justin Moon of South Korea is the world's top private eye. He travels to Singapore to catch an elusive cybercriminal. The pay is lucrative. His client is an attractive blonde CEO. It should be the easiest job in his career.

Things get complicated with the arrival of Okada, a mysterious drifter with a mission of revenge. As Moon tries to solve the mystery, he uncovers a tangled maze of deceit.

Each new clue leads him in an unpredictable direction. A deadly game of cat-and-mouse begins.

Featuring over 100 photos, *Edge of Suspicion* is both an exciting story and a work of art.

Envoy: Rule of Silence *by* ZITA STEELE

Take a journey into a thrilling world of secrets and lies in modern-day Europe. Polish ex-secret policeman Michal Krynski is tired of working as a double agent for France's security bureau.

His last mission: to track down a runaway DJ. As he travels to the strange island of Malta, Krynski plots revenge against the system that ruined his life.

Will he catch the DJ or kill him?

Zita Steele is a novelist and artist. She writes with an expertise in criminology, cybercrime, and international relations. She creates her own illustrations.

More Books from Fletcher & Co. Publishers

FLETCHER & CO. PUBLISHERS

Every book is a journey

Every book is a journey. Fletcher & Co. Publishers is an independent, art-house publishing company. We use new media and graphic design techniques to transport you into the world of the novel.

Our books aren't just written words. They're experiences: international cultures, art, suspense, history, and adventure.

Watch our video trailers on our YouTube and Vimeo channels to preview each book, see interesting images, and learn more about our newest releases. Visit us on our website or Facebook to find out about our latest news.

Coming Soon!

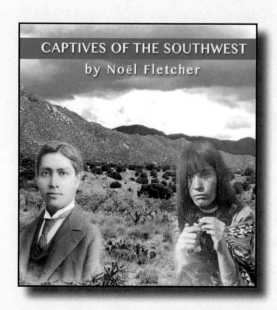

Captives of the Southwest
by Noël Fletcher

Take a journey back to the days of great struggles in the Wild West and explores the lives of Native Americans, Europeans and Hispanics who were taken away from their people.

The Strange Side of War *by* SARAH MACNAUGHTAN & NOËL FLETCHER

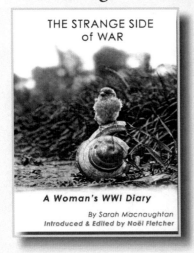

Take a journey across the dangerous battlefields of a world at war. Accompany Scottish novelist Sarah Macnaughtan as she volunteers alongside British humanitarian groups to alleviate the suffering in war-torn lands. Her many adventures tell unique stories of tragedy and triumph, taking readers on an unforgettable journey from the trenches of Belgium to the distant frontiers of Persia and tsarist Russia. Author/editor Noël Fletcher provides new historical context that brings Sarah's story to life and helps readers to remember the bravery and sacrifice of those who died. Illustrated with 130+ rare photos and propaganda posters from World War I, this important work features historical insights about the people and places involved in the conflict.

Lantern of the Wicked *by* CHARLES CLEMENT

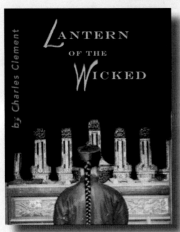

In the decadent and dangerous Shanghai of 1929, someone is spying for the Japanese, and the International Settlement's British police are on the hunt. Now, in the midst of the Mid-Autumn Moon Festival, American aviator Jack "Ace" Jordan becomes the prime suspect. A thrilling narrative blending fact, fiction and rare photographs, *Lantern of the Wicked* creates an atmospheric window into the complexity and dark grandeur of the colonial Orient in this gripping historical mystery.

New Mexico Ghosts and Haunting Images *by* ARIELA DESOLINA

Let explorer-photographer Ariela Desolina spirit you away to New Mexico, where haunting ruins - some with ghostly inhabitants - will capture your imagination. With photos from the St. James Hotel, a notorious hangout of Western outlaws and gamblers, and other mysterious locations. Mysterious shapes and ghostly forms (undetected when the pictures were taken) sometimes appear in her photos. This collection features photos of the notorious St. James Hotel in Cimarron, a famous haunt of outlaws and gamblers and the haunted ruins of the Kelly Mine, once among the richest old gold & silver mines in the Southwest.

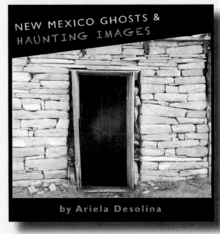

River of My Ancestors: The Rio Grande in Pictures *by* NOËL FLETCHER

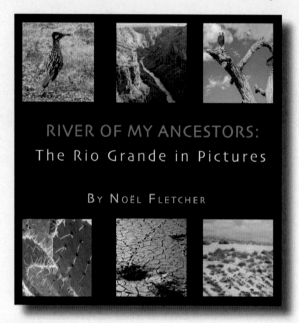

Take a journey along the wild and rugged Rio Grande. Beautiful pictures capture the essence of the famous river and its importance in the arid Southwest. Native New Mexican author and photographer Noël Fletcher provides family stories and insights about frontier life.

Follow the Rio Grande through deserts, wetlands, and rocky cliffs. Experience natural wonders, including volcanic lands and river rapids, and encounter wildlife such as snakes, wolves, cranes, and bighorn sheep.

With 180+ striking color photos, the book features:

- Author biography
- Wild West history
- Interesting facts about New Mexico, local culture, and life along the Rio Grande
- the world's largest cottonwood forest
- the legendary Rio Grande Gorge
- Spanish colonial irrigation systems
- Bosque del Apache National Wildlife Refuge
- Unique wildlife and plants
- Oral tradition from Spanish settlers and family stories

This captivating book combines vivid photos and the written word to tell a living history of the famous Rio Grande and the beautiful desert land of New Mexico.

Mystery of the Yellow Room The Spy *by* GASTON LEROUX

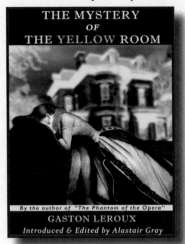

News of a strange crime spreads like wildfire in Paris. Someone has attempted to murder the daughter of a brilliant scientist. But nobody can explain how the murderer got in and out of the locked room of her isolated country home. Only Joseph Rouletabille, an impatient young journalist, has the genius to solve this crime. Written by the author of *"The Phantom of the Opera,"* this novel was published in 1907 as France's reply to Sherlock Holmes. Our edition has adapted text from archaic Victorian to standard English. It also features updated maps and is illustrated with 30+ historical paintings and illustrations from 19th century France.

The Spy *by* JAMES FENIMORE COOPER

During the dark days of the Revolutionary War, America struggles for nationhood. Meanwhile, in the shadows, a spy is trading secrets of vital importance to the cause – but for whose side? Colonials and loyalists play a game of cloak and daggers in a classic historical of action and adventure. Our edition features 30+ color photographs, chapter titles, and illuminating notations, designed to give you a front-seat experience. This was the first major fiction novel on espionage ever written and published in America.

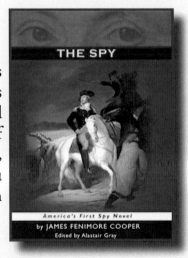

Two Years in the Forbidden City *by* PRINCESS DER LING

This true story was the first eyewitness account of the Imperial Court written by a Chinese aristocrat for Western readers. It provides an up-close view of the notorious Dowager Empress Tzu-hsi in her final years. Enhanced with rich imagery and additional historical notes, it includes interesting historical details and photos about China's infamous Dowager Empress, the Boxer Rebellion and the Imperial Court. It is illustrated with 100+ historical photographs, illustrations, and paintings from the late 1800s to early 1900s. Author/editor Noël Fletcher that provides context for this book in modern Chinese history.

Made in the USA
Monee, IL
21 November 2020